Published in 2009 and 2020 by Helen Exley®LONDON in Great Britain.

12 11 10 9 8 7 6 5 4 3 2 1

Selection and arrangement copyright © Helen Exley 2009, 2020. The moral right of the author has been asserted.

ISBN 978-1-84634-232-5

A copy of the CIP data is available from the British Library on request. All rights reserved.

No part of this publication may be reproduced or transmitted in any form or by any means, electronic or otherwise, without permission in writing from the publisher.

Edited by Dalton Exley.

Series Editor Helen Exley.

Printed in China.

Helen Exley® LONDON, 16 Chalk Hill, Watford, WD19 4BG, UK.
www.helenexley.com

THIS TOO WILL PASS

A HELEN EXLEY GIFTBOOK

The world is round and the place which ma

seem like the end may also be the beginning.

IVY BAKER PRIEST (1905-1975)

Stardust

We each hold within us a scrap of stardust,
a little glory that cannot be destroyed.
Whatever dark engulfs us, nothing can put out its light.

PAM BROWN, B.1928

"This too will pass..."

I was taught these words by my grandmother

(as a phrase that is to be used at all times in your life).

When things are spectacularly dreadful; when things are

absolutely appalling; when everything is superb

and wonderful and marvellous and happy –

say these four words to yourself.

They will give you a sense of perspective

and help you also to make sense of what is good

and to be stoical about what is bad.

CLAIRE RAYNER B.1931

each day a life...

EACH DAY THE FIRST DAY: EACH DAY A LIFE.

D. H. HAMMARSKJOLD (1905-1961)

Do not waste time on might-have-beens.
Today is your beginning.

CHARLOTTE GRAY

I like living.
I have sometimes been wildly,
despairingly,
acutely miserable,
racked with sorrow,
but through it all I still know
quite certainly
that just to be alive
is a grand thing.

AGATHA CHRISTIE
(1890-1976)

Deep in the soul, below pain,

below all the distraction of life,

is a silence vast and grand —

an infinite ocean of calm,

which nothing can disturb;

nature's own exceeding peace,

which "passes understanding".

That which we seek

with passionate longing,

here and there,

upward and outward;

we find at last within ourselves.

R.M. BUCKE (1837-1902)

The only way out is through.

HELEN KELLER (1880-1968)

Turn your face to the sun and the shadows fall behind you.

MAORI PROVERB

Rest in patience.
Above the storm the sky is clear
and strewn with silent stars.

PAM BROWN, B.1928

When you have gone so far
that you can't manage
one more step,
then you've gone just
half the distance
that you're capable of.

GREENLAND PROVERB

Joy and sorrow are life's
companions.

JAPANESE PROVERB

Even when I'm sick and depressed, I love life.

ARTHUR RUBINSTEIN

...Misfortune and destruction are not final.

When the grass has been burnt

by the fire of the steppe,

it will grow anew in summer.

MONGOLIAN WISDOM

Do not weep; do not wax indignant. Understand.

WILLIAM JAMES (1842-1910)

Linked by love

You are yourself

and yet you are a part of humankind

– linked by love and joy and sorrow.

Millions upon millions have known this grief you suffer.

In this, each is brought closer to their kin

– whatever their time and place in history,

whatever their race or creed or circumstance.

PAM BROWN, B.1928

Sorrow can shut us away from those who love us.

Reach out and take their hands.

Here is life and love

and the promise of better days.

PETER GRAY

Take their hands...

In the end possessions mean nothing,

ambition is a childish fantasy.

Even beauty blurs —

so that all things come together in a new perception.

And only love is left.

CHARLOTTE GRAY

only love is left...

A kind word to one in trouble
is often like a switch
in a railroad track...
an inch between wreck and
smooth sailing.

HENRY WARD BEECHER (1813-1887)

A kind word...

It is the small, insignificant, simple gestures
that make life bearable.
A smile, a touch, a word, a kindness,
a concern.

PAM BROWN, B.1928

It is a terrible thing, this kindness that human beings do not lose.
Terrible because when we are finally naked in the dark and cold,
it is all we have. We who are so rich, so full of strength, wind up
with that small change. We have nothing else to give.

URSULA K. LE GUIN, B.1929

The compassionate person
understands that there is a time
for talk and a time for silence.

PABLO CASALS (1876-1973)

There is kindness
in the world —
and wisdom and
courtesy and love.
In city tenements,
in deserts,
forests, villages —
in this town.
This street.
Never forget.

PAM BROWN, B.1928

give

It is only when we have descended to the depths of sorrow
that we can understand the complexity of being human,
feel for all other suffering living creatures,
— and give understanding, kindness, and companionship
to those who need it.

PAM BROWN, B.1928

The shock and failure of disappointments, of betrayal, hits like a physical blow. Breathless and blinded, you lose all contact with the life you lived till now — the ordinary life that seemed untouchable. Hold fast. However impossible it seems that happiness and certainty will return — they will, they will....

PAM BROWN, B.1928

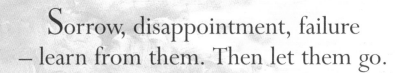

Sorrow, disappointment, failure
– learn from them. Then let them go.

CHARLOTTE GRAY

It's a good thing to have all the props pulled out from under us occasionally.
It gives us some sense of what is rock under our feet, and what is sand.

MADELEINE L'ENGLE (1918-2007)

WE OUGHT TO REMEMBER

THAT WE ARE NOT THE ONLY ONES

TO FIND OURSELVES

AT AN APPARENT IMPASSE.

JUST AS A KITE RISES AGAINST THE WIND,

EVEN THE WORST OF TROUBLES

CAN STRENGTHEN US.

AS THOUSANDS BEFORE US

HAVE MET THE IDENTICAL FATE AND MASTERED IT,

SO CAN WE!

DR. R. BRASCH

Never bear more than one kind of trouble at a time. Some people bear three — all they have had, all they have now, and all they expect to have.

EDWARD E. HALE (1822-1909)

You have to accept whatever comes and the only important thing is that you meet it with courage and the best you have to give.

ELEANOR ROOSEVELT (1884-1962)

…trust life

…life catches up with us
and teaches us to love and forgive each other.

JUDY COLLINS B.1939

It had been my repeated experience

that when you said to life calmly and firmly

(but very firmly!)

"I trust you; do what you must,"

life had an uncanny way of responding to your need.

OLGA ILYIN

There is a wisdom at the heart of things.
And we, frail, silly, frightened creatures that we are,
are part of it.

Do not be afraid.

PETER GRAY

Life could not continue,

without throwing the past into the past,

liberating the present from its burden.

PAUL TILLICH (1886-1965)

Hope is necessary in every condition.

The miseries of poverty, sickness of captivity would,

without this comfort, be insupportable.

DR. SAMUEL JOHNSON (1709-1784)

acceptance

Acceptance of what has happened is the first step to overcoming the consequences of any misfortune....

WILLIAM JAMES (1842-1910)

There is nothing to be gained by wishing you were someplace else or waiting for a better situation. You see where you are and you do what you can with that.

JACOB K. JAVITS (1904-1986)

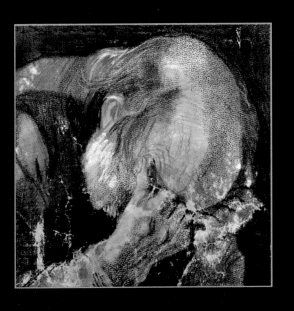

Some sorrows leave an emptiness,

a gap in time,

a loved place where one can no longer go.

Remember that you need time.

To share. To weep.

To help you move on.

Listen to sorrow.

Choose your own way of healing.

Give yourself time.

PAM BROWN, B.1928

Listen...

Analyzing the causes of anguish is effort wasted.

There is no going back.

No spell can change what has happened,

no blaming this or that.

Whenever you're deeply troubled,

persuade your mind to concentrate on little,

present pleasures.

Give yourself time to heal. Be still.

CHARLOTTE GRAY

Recovery is a process, not an event.

ANNE WILSON SCHAEF

One of the best safeguards

of our hopes,

I have suggested,

is to be able to mark off

the areas of hopelessness

and to acknowledge them,

to face them directly,

not with despair

but with the creative intent

of keeping them from polluting

all the areas of possibility.

WILLIAM F. LYNCH (1801-1865)

Time...

There is no certain cure for sorrow.

Various tinctures may help you

— friendship, occupation, change —

But all must be taken in a solution of time.

PAM BROWN, B.1928

Real courage:

The great virtue in life is real courage that knows
how to face facts and live beyond them.

D.H.LAWRENCE (1885-1930)

Courage is, with love, the greatest gift.

We are, each of us, defeated many times —

but we accept defeat and learn from it,

and try another way —

then we will find peace, and

in the end, fulfilment.

ROSANNE AMBROSE BROWN

The greatest gift...

No matter how dark things seem to be
or actually are, raise your sights
and see the possibilities —
always see them, for they're always there.

NORMAN VINCENT PEALE (1898-1993)

We shall draw from the heart of suffering
the means of inspiration and survival.

SIR WINSTON CHURCHILL (1874-1965)

To endure is greater than to dare;

to tire out hostile fortune;

to be daunted by no difficulty;

to keep heart when all have lost it —

who can say this is not greatness?

WILLIAM MAKEPEACE THACKERAY
(1811-1863)

Keep heart...

*O*ut *of suffering have emerged the strongest souls,*

the most massive characters are seamed with scars....

E.H. CHAPIN (1814-1880)

*O*ut of every crisis comes the chance to be reborn,

to reconceive ourselves as individuals,

to choose the kind of change that will help us to grow

and to fulfil ourselves more completely.

NENA O'NEILL (1923-2006)

There is a quiet place inside you that no torment can touch.
Wait for however long is needed, in that stillness, until the storm passes.

MAYA V. PATEL

It isn't for the moment you are struck that you need courage,
but for the long uphill climb back to sanity and faith and security.

ANNE MORROW LINDBERGH (1906-2001)

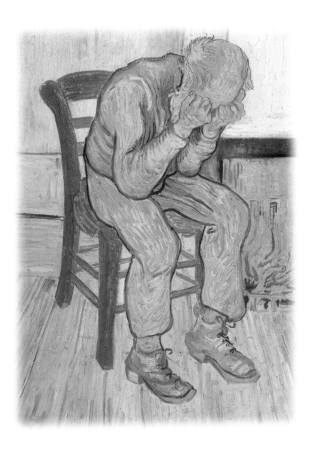

The more we love,
the more we sorrow at its loss —
by circumstance or distance or by death.
Yet it is never really lost.
It has changed us forever.

In great sorrow,
despite kind words and outstretched arms,
we stand alone.
We must walk the maze of desolation on our own
— and by our own courage
find at last freedom and the light of living.

PAM BROWN, B.1928

We are healed from suffering only
by experiencing it to the full.

MARCEL PROUST (1871-1922)

Don't be sad,
don't be angry, disappointed!
Submit to your grief –
your time for joy will come,
believe me.

ALEKSANDR SERGEYEVICH PUSHKIN
(1799-1837)

We perceive that only
through utter defeat are we
able to take our first steps
towards liberation and strength.
Our admissions of
personal powerlessness
finally turn out to be
a firm bedrock
upon which happy and
purposeful lives may be built.

BILL WILSON (1895-1971)

Always we hope someone else has the answer.
Some other place will be better,
some other time it will all turn out well,
This is it.
No one else has the answer.
No other place will be better,
and it has already turned out.
At the centre of your being
you have the answer;
you know who you are
and you know what you want.

LAO TZU, FROM "TAO TE CHING"

Our remedies oft in ourselves do lie.

WILLIAM SHAKESPEARE (1564-1616)

Just be

Such words as "death" and "suffering"
and "eternity" are best forgotten.
We have to become as simple and as wordless
as the growing corn or the falling rain.
We must just be.

ETTY HILLESUM (1914-1943)

Time's healing touch...

Though now you are bereft and ways seem black,

With emptiness and gloom on every hand;

Someday Time's healing touch will lead you back,

And gradually your heart will understand

That what you bore must come to one and all...

...And Peace, the clean white flower born of pain,

Will slowly, surely, rise from sorrow's pall,

And happiness will come to you again.

MARGARET E. BRUNER (1886-1970)

Start again...

When you feel

that you have reached the end

and that you cannot go one step further,

when life seems to be drained

of all purpose:

What a wonderful opportunity

to start all over again,

to turn over a new page.

EILEEN CADDY

Hope...

Every area of trouble gives out a ray of hope,
and the one unchangeable certainty
is that nothing is certain or unchangeable.

JOHN F. KENNEDY (1917-1963)

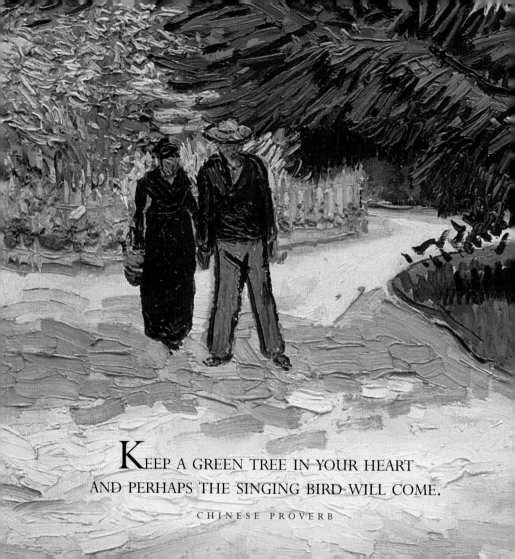

Keep a green tree in your heart
and perhaps the singing bird will come.

CHINESE PROVERB

Healing is simply attempting to do more of those things that bring joy and fewer of those things that bring pain.

DR. O. CARL SIMONTON (1942-2009)

It's better to light a candle than to curse the darkness.

ELEANOR ROOSEVELT (1884-1962)

Sorrow is the touchstone of love.
Love that can understand and share
is love that will endure and grow.
Love that can only live in joy is ephemeral.

PAM BROWN, B.1928

DIFFICULTIES ARE THE THINGS THAT SHOW WHAT WE ARE.

EPICTETUS

H old on; hold fast; hold out. Patience is genius.

COMTE DE BUFFON

And the miracle is:
if you can go into your suffering as a meditation,
watching, to the deepest roots of it,
just through watching, it disappears.
You don't have to do anything more than watching.
If you have found the authentic cause by your watching,
the suffering will disappear.

OSHO (1931-1990)

To wish to be well is a part of becoming well.

SENECA (C.4 B.C. - C.65 A.D.)

$\mathbf{I}$t has never been, and never will be easy work!

But the road that is built in hope is more pleasant

to the traveler than the road built in despair,

even though they both lead to the same destination.

MARION ZIMMER BRADLEY (1930-1999)

live every moment

To be able to set grief aside it may be necessary to live
every moment again and again, dissect and analyse and rediscover.
Until at last the heart allows the past to be accepted as a memory
– and life can go on.

PETER GRAY

Strengthen me by sympathizing with my strength,
not my weakness.

A. BRONSON ALCOTT

(1799-1888)

God grant me the serenity to accept the things I cannot change,

courage to change the things I can,

and wisdom to know the difference.

REINHOLD NIEBUHR (1892-1971)
FROM "THE SERENITY PRAYER"

let it go

The past is done with

– all the mistakes, all the disappointments.

Let them go.

There is nothing you can change.

But nothing is ever wasted.

All of it was learning.

Make good use of it.

CHARLOTTE GRAY

Loss leaves us empty –

but learn not to close your heart and mind in grief.

Allow life to replenish you.

When sorrow comes it seems impossible –

but new joys wait to fill the void.

CHARLOTTE GRAY

Never give up...

When you get into a tight place and everything goes against you,

till it seems as though you could not hang on a minute longer,

never give up then, for that is just the place and time

that the tide will turn.

HARRIET BEECHER STOWE (1811-1896)

Infinite hope...

W<small>E MUST ACCEPT FINITE DISAPPOINTMENT,</small>

<small>BUT WE MUST NEVER LOSE INFINITE HOPE.</small>

MARTIN LUTHER KING, JR
(1929 - 1968)

*P*ut the sad things of the past behind you –

The disappointments, the mistakes, the embarrassments.

All that brought you sorrow and regret.

Learn from them and let them go.

PAM BROWN, B.1928

Birds sing after a storm,
why shouldn't people feel as free to delight
in whatever remains to them?

ROSE KENNEDY (1890-1995)

free to delight...

the birds still sing...

The sky is still as blue,

The grass is still as green,

The birds sing as sweetly,

The flowers have not lost their fragrance.

It may not seem so at the moment but slowly it will.

STUART AND LINDA MACFARLANE

Pain is temporary. It may last a minute,
or an hour, or a day, or a year,
but eventually it will subside
and something else will take its place.

LANCE ARMSTRONG, B.1971

In the depth of winter, I finally learned
that within me there lay an invincible summer.

ALBERT CAMUS (1913 - 1960)

I am emerging from an ocean of grief.

From the sorrow of many deaths.

From the inevitability of tragedy.

From the losing of love,

From the terrible triumph of destruction.

I am seeing the living that is to be lived,

The laughter that is to be laughed,

The joy that is to be enjoyed,

The loving that is to be accomplished.

I am learning at last

The tremendous triumph of life.

MARJORIE PIZER, B.1920
"TRIUMPH OF LIFE"

Oh, you grief-stricken,

...in the end the bubble of your grief

shall be swept away

in the ocean of peacefulness.

RABINDRANATH TAGORE (1861-1941)

Though nothing can bring back the hour

Of splendour in the grass, of glory in the flower;

We will grieve not, rather find

Strength in what remains behind.

WILLIAM WORDSWORTH (1770-1850)

The beauty that remains...

I don't think of all the misery, but of the beauty that still remains.

ANNE FRANK (1929-1945)

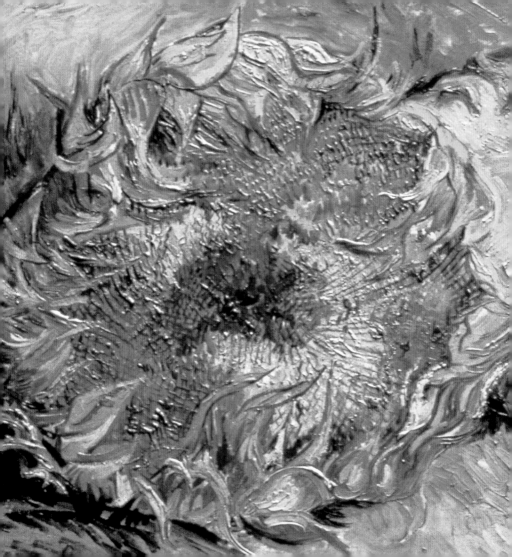